1 MONTH OF
FREE
READING

at
www.ForgottenBooks.com

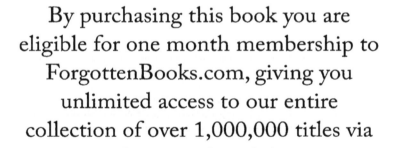

By purchasing this book you are eligible for one month membership to ForgottenBooks.com, giving you unlimited access to our entire collection of over 1,000,000 titles via our web site and mobile apps.

To claim your free month visit:
www.forgottenbooks.com/free1117616

ISBN 978-0-331-39439-9
PIBN 11117616

For support please visit www.forgottenbooks.com

S. D. A. Forest Service   1969
source Bulletin INT-8

FORESTS IN SOUTH DAKOTA

By

Grover A. Choate

and

John S. Spencer, Jr.

North Central Forest Experiment Station
David B. King, Director St. Paul, Minnesota 55101

Rocky Mountain Forest and Range Experiment Station
Raymond Price, Director   Fort Collins, Colorado 80521

Intermountain Forest and Range Experiment Station
Joseph F. Pechanec, Director   Ogden, Utah 84401

FOREST SERVICE / U. S. DEPARTMENT OF AGRICULTURE

THE AUTHORS

Grover A. Choate has written similar reports describing forest resources in many of the Rocky Mountain States. Before coming to the Intermountain Forest and Range Experiment Station he had broad experience in forest and land-use inventories as well as in research in aerial photo techniques. His previous experience was in the Lake States, Pacific Northwest, Washington, D. C., and Southeast Asia.

John S. Spencer, Jr., is presently a resource analyst in the North Central Forest Experiment Station at St. Paul, Minnesota. His previous Forest Service experience was on National Forests in Montana and California and at the Intermountain Forest and Range Experiment Station, Ogden, Utah. He has written or coauthored several reports on forest resources and timber production in the Rocky Mountain States.

FOREWORD

This report presents the most recent statistics on South Dakota's forest area and timber volumes, growth, removals, and industries. It also makes certain broad comparisons with the forest situation as reported in 1936 (Ware),[1] indicates recent trends in inventory and use of timber, and projects growth, cut, and inventory to 1992. In short, it provides much of the information necessary for long-range planning of the timber resource.

The 1936 survey was designed primarily to determine the proper relation of farm forestry to other phases of farm management. Both the 1936 report and this report are based on inventories conducted by several administrative units of the U. S. D. A. Forest Service as part of its continuing nationwide Forest Survey program. Collection of statistics for this report began in 1960 and was completed in 1965. Thus, tables in this report are dated 1962 because that year was near the middle of this collection period.

Differences in inventory and utilization standards between the inventory reported in 1936 and the one reported here handicap comparisons of statistics from the two surveys. However, broad comparisons have been made after first adjusting (as much as possible) figures on total area, volume, growth, and removals in the 1936 report to meet current standards.

A discussion of trends in recent years (1952-67) is based on results of backdating new survey data to 1952 and updating to 1967.

Many of the statistics shown in this report do not agree with those shown in the last two national timber appraisals. Statistics for 1952 used in the trend discussion, which are based on the stand table backdating of the new survey as indicated above, are considered more realistic than those reported in Timber Resources for America's Future (U. S. Forest Serv. 1958). Because some tables in this new report include data collected since 1962, they will not agree with corresponding 1962 tables shown in Timber Trends in the United States (U. S. Forest Serv. 1965).

---

[1] *Names and dates in parentheses refer to Literature Cited, p. 15.*

Many of the statistics shown in this report are a composite of those already published separately for eastern and western South Dakota (Caporaso 1964; Spencer et al. 1964; Chase 1967).

Inventory data for western South Dakota[2] were collected during 1960 as a cooperative effort of the Rocky Mountain Region (Region 2) and the Intermountain Forest and Range Experiment Station. Data for eastern South Dakota were collected between December 1964 and April 1965 by the North Central Forest Experiment Station. A survey of timber removals, products output, and industries in western South Dakota for 1962 was made by the Intermountain Station, and in eastern South Dakota for 1964 by the North Central Station.

The Appendix to this report should be consulted for definitions of terms, survey methods and reliability of data, and detailed timber statistics. Next to the inside back cover is a generalized forest type map of South Dakota.

---

[2]*Includes all of Harding, Butte, Lawrence, and Fall River Counties as well as all lands west of the 103d meridian in Meade, Pennington, and Custer Counties.*

ii

CONTENTS

STATISTICAL HIGHLIGHTS

FOREST AREA

- The forest area covers 1.7 million acres, or 3.5 percent of South Dakota's land area.
- Commercial forests cover 1.5 million acres, or 89 percent of the forest area. The commercial forest area decreased 8 percent between 1935 and 1962.
- 72 percent of the commercial forest area is publicly owned. The U. S. D. A. Forest Service administers 62 percent of this area.
- 53 percent of the commercial forest area is in sawtimber stands; these stands average 3,840 board feet per acre.[3]
- The ponderosa pine type occupies 87 percent of the commercial area; the remainder is largely hardwood types.
- About 8 percent of the commercial forest area has a sustainable yield potential of more than 50 cubic feet per acre a year. The average annual potential for the total commercial forest area is 36 cubic feet per acre.

TIMBER VOLUME

- Commercial forests have 1.1 billion cubic feet of wood in all sound, live trees, and 3.7 billion board feet in sound, live trees of sawtimber size.
- Cubic-foot inventory increased about 50 percent between 1935 and 1962; sawtimber inventory remained about the same.

---

[3]*International ¼-inch log rule board-foot volumes are used throughout this report unless otherwise stated.*

- 79 percent of the sawtimber volume is publicly owned.
- Seven-eighths of the sawtimber volume is ponderosa pine.

STAND CONDITIONS

- Mortality was low; only 7 percent of gross growth of growing stock and a slightly lower percentage of sawtimber growth were offset by mortality.
- Diseases accounted for 56 percent of the growing stock mortality during 1962.

TIMBER USE

- South Dakota's timber cut of 13.3 million cubic feet from growing stock in 1962 was 1.2 percent of inventory.
- 48 percent of the volume of roundwood products cut in 1962 was saw logs for lumber; 22 percent was pulpwood.
- During the period 1952-67, volume of timber harvested increased at an average rate of 3 percent per year.
- National Forest percentage of the total cut from growing stock in the State increased from 45 percent in 1935 to 82 percent in 1962.

THE FOREST SITUATION TODAY

South Dakota's forest lands — 1.7 million acres comprising about 3.5 percent of the area of the State — are of increasing significance for timber, recreation, water, and other values. The economic and social benefits of these lands extend well beyond the borders of the State. About 1.5 million acres, or 89 percent of the forest land, are classed as commercially important for timber production. Products from timberlands — lumber, mine timber, poles, posts, and others — were originally marketed mainly in South Dakota and adjoining States; but many of these products as well as pulpwood now have moved to more distant markets in the Midwest. Recreation use of forest lands has increased very rapidly. State, federal, and private facilities have been pressed to meet mounting local and tourist demands for a wide variety of outdoor recreation opportunities. Water yields, particularly from the relatively high and heavily forested area of the Black Hills, are significant in this semiarid part of the country. Forest lands also provide important habitat for many wildlife species.

Nearly 200,000 acres of forest land are classed as noncommercial from the standpoint of timber yields. Ninety percent of this area is unproductive, either because site conditions are too poor to grow commercial crops of trees for industry, or because the forest type currently occupying the land is comprised of juniper, scrub hardwoods, or similar vegetation not of commercial importance for wood products at this time. The remaining 10 percent of the noncommercial area, although capable of growing commercial timber, is reserved for other use.

Commercial Forest Area

Forests in South Dakota represent a transition from hardwoods (broadleaf trees) of the plains in the east to the predominantly soft-wood (evergreen) forests of the Rocky Mountains to the west. The woodlands of the eastern part of the State (roughly east of Rapid City) consist mainly of natural stands of such native species as cottonwood, ash, elm, and oak. Some natural stands of hardwoods occur on upland sites, but are most common along streams, lakes, and reservoirs. Shelterbelt plantations of native and introduced species are also widely scattered throughout the rolling farmland areas of eastern South Dakota.

Ponderosa pine is by far the predominant species in the western part of the State. As a timber type it occupies 1,352,000 acres of which 1,330,000 acres is commercial forest. The latter figure represents about 87 percent of the State's commercial forest area. White spruce also occurs as a commercial timber type in western South Dakota although the area it occupies is very small — 23,000 acres.

The Black Hills support the State's most significant commercial timber resource — extensive areas of ponderosa pine. The Black Hills lie within Lawrence, Meade, Pennington, Custer, and Fall River Counties, and these counties account for more than 85 percent of the commercial forest area of the State. This uplift area, where elevations range from about 3,200 to 7,242 feet above mean sea level, has the precipitation and other site conditions that permit the occurrence of ponderosa pine.

Few eastern South Dakota counties have more than 1 percent of their area in commercial forest. Union County in the southeastern corner of the State is the only one with more than 2 percent (see page 4).

Sawtimber stands occupy 813,000 acres and poletimber stands occupy 637,000 acres; combined they comprise 95 percent of the commercial forest area. A very small area (19,000 acres) is classed as nonstocked.

Water and recreation, along with timber, forage for domestic livestock, and wildlife habitat, are all sign
values derived from South Dakota's forests. As demands on the forest lands have increased — especially
World War II — management for multiple uses has been intensified. Recreation visits have mounted ra
Statistics on such visits to National Forest facilities indicate that 1964 visits in South Dakota we
times the number in 1946, as compared with 2.4 times for all National Forests countrywide. The swi
beach shown here is at Sheridan Lake on the Black Hills National Forest. This manmade reservoir, which is
runoff from forest lands, also provides a relatively stable supply of water for use and reuse by downs
consumers. Such developed sites are among the many features that attract more visitors each year to the
Hills National Forest than to any other National Forest in the country.

significant
ncially since
ed rapidly.
e were 28
swimming
sh is fed by
anstream
o the Back

Ponderosa pine stands, such as the one shown here in the Black Hills, predominate on 1.3 million acres of commercial forests — nearly 7 out of every 8 acres of commercial forest land in the State. Almost one-third of the growing stock volume is in trees between 5.0 and 8.9 inches in diameter at breast height (d.b.h.) and 92 percent in trees between 5.0 and 18.9 inches d.b.h. Sites are relatively poor for this species in South Dakota compared to most of the areas on which ponderosa pine occurs throughout the West; trees average about 35 feet in height at 50 years of age. However, reproduction is usually abundant in ponderosa pine stands in the Black Hills that have been opened up. This is illustrated in the photograph which shows a heavily overstocked understory of saplings beneath scattered poletimber trees that are about 45 feet high and 120 years old. At least one precommercial thinning is desirable before trees reach merchantable size for posts or plywood.

3

Forest and Nonforest land areas by county groupings, 1962

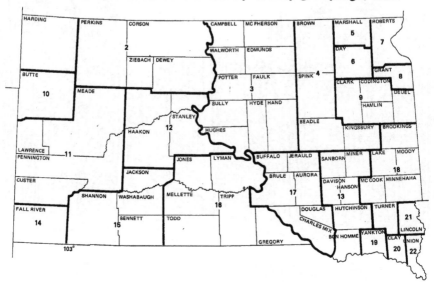

No. on map	All land[1]	Nonforest land	Total forest land	Land Class	
				Commercial	Noncommercial
			Thousand acres		
1	1,717	1,701	16	15	1
2	5,225	5,205	20	14	6
3	6,265	6,249	16	10	6
4	3,368	3,355	13	10	3
5	560	554	6	5	1
6	678	675	3	3	([2])
7	711	695	16	13	3
8	438	433	5	4	1
9	1,807	1,801	6	5	1
10	1,441	1,429	12	5	7
11	5,499	4,179	1,320	1,235	85
12	3,142	3,129	13	10	3
13	2,166	2,154	12	9	3
14	1,114	1,011	103	76	27
15	3,300	3,233	67	45	22
16	5,090	5,036	54	36	18
17	2,615	2,607	8	5	3
18	2,495	2,475	20	16	4
19	333	328	5	4	1
20	258	254	4	3	1
21	369	365	4	3	1
22	291	281	10	8	2
Total	48,882	47,149	1,733	1,534	199

[1] *From Bureau of the Census, 1960.*
[2] *Less than 500 acres.*

4

The bulk of the commercial forest area is in public ownership:

	Percent
National Forest	63
Other federal	5
State	4
Private	28

There is considerable difference between softwood and hardwood areas with respect to ownership. Nearly four-fifths of the softwood area is publicly owned, the other one-fifth privately. In the case of hardwoods, the situation is reversed with four-fifths in private ownership.

About 99 percent of the 957,000 acres of commercial forest area in National Forest ownership is in the Black Hills National Forest, which straddles the Wyoming border. The remaining 1 percent is in the Custer National Forest in Harding County.

Timber Volume

Ninety-seven percent of the 1.12 billion cubic feet of timber on commercial forest lands is in growing stock trees; i.e., sound live trees 5 inches and larger in diameter at breast height (d.b.h.); the remainder is in rough,

rotten, and salvable dead trees. However, the hardwood volume (0.1 billion cubic feet) has a substantial volume in defective trees — 26 percent.

Growing stock volume is largely in trees of sawtimber size and of softwood species. A little more than two-thirds of this volume is in sawtimber trees. Distribution of growing stock volume by species is as follows:

	Million Cubic feet	Percent
Ponderosa pine	961	88.6
White spruce	46	4.2
Cottonwood	28	2.6
Ash	19	1.7
Elm	16	1.5
Other	15	1.4
	1,085	100.0

There are no important differences from the above in the distribution by species of the 3.7 billion board feet of sawtimber volume.

In comparison with averages for the Rocky Mountain States,[4] sawtimber trees are rela-

[4] *The following are called Rocky Mountain or Mountain States in this report: Idaho, Montana, South Dakota (west of the 103d meridian), Wyoming, Colorado, Utah, Nevada, Arizona, and New Mexico.*

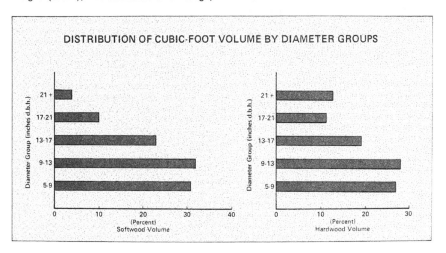

DISTRIBUTION OF CUBIC-FOOT VOLUME BY DIAMETER GROUPS

tively small in diameter in South Dakota and volumes per acre are low. Only 15 percent of the board-foot volume in South Dakota is in trees 19 inches d.b.h. and larger; this compares with nearly 40 percent for the Rocky Mountain area as a whole. Sawtimber volume per acre of commercial forest land in South Dakota is 2,422 board feet compared with an average of 6,276 board feet for the Mountain States and 4,985 for the United States. Sawtimber stands in South Dakota average 3,840 board feet per acre.

Distribution of growing stock of softwoods and hardwoods by tree diameter groups is illustrated by the chart on page 5.

The percentage of sawtimber volume among the four log grades used in the survey differs substantially between softwoods and hardwoods.[5] Only 2 percent of the softwood volume is in log grade 1; 83 percent is in grade 4. The majority (54 percent) of the hardwood volume is in grade 3 with the remainder fairly equally distributed among the other three grades.

The preponderance of timber volume is in National Forest ownership. The following percentage distribution by owners applies to both growing stock and sawtimber volume of all species combined:

	Percent
National Forest	72
Other public	7
Private	21

The distribution of softwood volumes is about the same as the above. However, more than 80 percent of the hardwood volume is privately owned, and only an insignificant amount is in National Forest ownership.

Growth and Mortality

In 1962 net annual growth amounted to 30 million cubic feet (including 103 million board feet sawtimber growth). These estimates represent the net increment after sub-

[5] *Different log grade standards are used for softwoods than for hardwoods; see Terminology in the Appendix.*

tracting average annual mortality from gross growth. Mortality amounted to about 2 million cubic feet for growing stock and 6 million board feet for sawtimber. In 1962 diseases were responsible for 56 percent of the growing stock mortality.

Estimates of annual net growth of growing stock indicated above are about 2.9 percent greater than the average for the 10 years preceding the survey. Mortality estimates are 28 percent less. These differences arise in large measure from the fact that estimated mortality for 1962 in the eastern part of the State is the average of only 3 years — years during which rainfall was greater and growing conditions better than the 10-year average. Differences are less for sawtimber.

Normal mortality losses per acre are low in South Dakota in relation to much of the commercial forest area of the country. South Dakota's annual loss of 1.4 cubic feet per acre is less than one-tenth the average for the Mountain States and is about one-eighth that of the United States. Sawtimber losses are also low. There can be many reasons for this low mortality, and misleading conclusions can be drawn from comparisons such as indicated above unless all factors are known and considered. Nevertheless, there is little doubt that relatively intensive management and utilization of the major component of the forest (ponderosa pine) tends to minimize mortality. This in turn is a factor in the State's relatively high rate of net growth for growing stock — 2.8 percent.

Another reason for low normal mortality is that forest fires are not as extensive as in many other areas. Sampling on the latest inventory did not reveal any mortality by fire on commercial forest land — although fires have occurred every year. Over the period 1953-64 South Dakota had an average of 182 fires a year on all (commercial and noncommercial) forest lands. However, the average size of fires in South Dakota was 35 acres in comparison with about 45 acres for a 12-State area in the Rocky Mountains and Great Plains. The average for the United States (exclusive of Alaska and Hawaii) was also about 45 acres. During the same period, only 0.13 percent of the forest area in need of protection was burned in South Dakota; this compares with 0.19 percent for the 12-State area mentioned above and 0.83 percent for the United States.

Timber Removals

Removals from growing stock in 1962 amounted to 13 million cubic feet (including 59 million board feet from sawtimber trees). Of these removals, 94 percent went into roundwood products (saw logs, pulpwood, fuelwood, poles, posts, etc.), and the remainder was mainly logging residues in the form of unused portions of trees cut or killed in logging. A small volume also resulted from thinnings, clearing for right-of-way construction, and changes in land use.

Distribution of removals from growing stock by ownership classes was as follows:

	Percent
National Forest	82
Other public	2
Private	16

Volume cut from growing stock for timber products, together with logging residues, amounted to 1.2 percent of the 1.1 billion cubic feet of growing stock inventory. Although this is less than the average for the United States (1.6 percent), it is higher than the average for any of the individual Mountain States or the average of 0.7 percent for the Mountain States area (Wilson and Spencer 1967).

The total output of timber products from all forest lands in 1962 amounted to 14.5 million cubic feet.[6] About 95 percent of this was roundwood products, the remainder was pulp chips and other plant byproducts. A little more than 90 percent of the roundwood products came from growing stock trees, the remainder from rough, rotten, and dead trees on commercial forests and from trees on lands not classified as commercial forest.

[6]*Includes material removed from noncommercial as well as commercial forest land, and from nongrowing stock as well as growing stock. It also includes plant byproducts.*

Forty-two million board feet of logs for lumber and hardwood veneer and 41,000 cords of pulpwood made up more than 70 percent of the total products output. In cubic measure, the output by various products was as follows:

Thousand cubic feet

Saw logs	6,658
Veneer logs	199
Pulpwood	3,564
Piling	10
Poles	570
Posts	833
Fuelwood	2,041
Other	605
All products	**14,480**

Except for pulpwood, which was all shipped to mills in the Lake States, the great majority of the volume of all other products was cut for wood processing plants located within South Dakota. About 7 million board feet of logs were shipped to Wyoming but this was more than offset by 8.5 million board feet brought in from Wyoming.

The largest sawmill in South Dakota shown here is at Spearfish and is owned by the Homestake Mining Company; it has an annual capacity of about 17 million board feet. About one-half of the production is lumber; the remainder is mine timbers, snow fence lathe, and chips. The company's substantial timber holdings in the Black Hills are under forward-looking management for sustained yields.

TRENDS IN SUPPLY AND USE

The importance of South Dakota's forests as well as timber products to the State and other Midwest areas has resulted in many changes in the timber situation over the years. These changes appear particularly great in comparison with many other States in the midcontinent area, especially in relation to the Rocky Mountain area.

Although forest area has been somewhat reduced since 1935 because of impingement by other land uses, the supply situation has been greatly improved. Timber volumes, growth, and product harvest have all increased substantially over the last few decades. Most of this improvement results from more intensive protection and management of the State's major timber resource — the ponderosa pine lands. Establishment of the Black Hills National Forest in 1897 was a significant landmark in getting forests in this area under scientific management. In fact, the first regulated cutting on National Forests anywhere in the country began on the Black Hills National Forest a year after it was established. Now, with the holdings of the Homestake Mining Company and the State of South Dakota under management similar to that of the National Forests, essentially all the forests of the Black Hills are managed with the objective of a high level of sustained yield.

During the period 1935-62, the area of commercial forest dropped from 1,674,600 to 1,534,000 acres — a decrease of 140,600 acres.[7] This reduction occurred largely in eastern South Dakota because of flooding of wooded areas by reservoirs along the Missouri River and adjacent portions of tributaries. However, some reduction has occurred throughout the State because of changes in land use and right-of-way clearing.

Growing stock inventory increased from 720 million cubic feet in 1935 to 1,085

[7]*Estimates for 1935 used for comparisons in this report have been adjusted as much as possible in light of changes in inventory and utilization standards between inventories.*

million cubic feet in 1962 — roughly 50 percent. Sawtimber inventory remained about the same. Decreases of 43 percent in both cubic- and board-foot volumes in the eastern part of the State were more than offset by increases in the western part of the State — particularly in cubic volume, which increased 77 percent. For the State, the volume of hardwood growing stock decreased nearly 50 percent while that of softwood increased 77 percent.

The flooding of timber areas not only caused substantial reduction in forest area, but it also was undoubtedly the major reason for the drop in timber volumes in the eastern part of the State.

Droughts since 1930 have also affected timberlands, particularly in the eastern part of the State. Although the 1950's were dry, the most severe period was the 1930's when average precipitation in 9 out of the 10 years was below the 18-inch annual average for the period 1930-62. Mortality, as a result of drought, was undoubtedly a factor in reducing inventory in eastern South Dakota, and in limiting the amount of net growth. However, despite the depressing effect of drought a substantial increase in net annual growth undoubtedly occurred. Reliable data are not available for the amount of net growth in 1935, but evidence suggests that net growth for the State in 1962 (30 million cubic feet) was in the neighborhood of 2.9 times the amount in 1935.

Although the volume of timber cut from growing stock in the course of harvesting only increased from 12 million cubic feet in 1935 to 13 million in 1962, significant changes have occurred within the timber industry. In 1935 only about 45 percent of the timber cut from growing stock came from National Forest lands; in 1962 it amounted to 82 percent. The product mix also changed to an important degree between 1935 and 1962. The following tabulation indicates the breakdown of cubic-foot volume of products from all sources for the 2 years.

1935[1]	Percent	1962	Percent
Saw logs	57.5	Saw logs[2]	47.4
Fuelwood	40.2	Fuelwood	14.1
Posts	2.3	Pulpwood	24.6
		Other	13.9

[1]Estimates of product volumes given in the 1936 report (Ware) are actually based on averages of annual estimates for the period 1924-34; it is assumed here that these averages can be used for 1935.

[2]Includes a small volume of hardwood veneer logs.

Production of pulp chips from residues of saw log production has become a significant factor in pulpwood production. In 1962 pulp chips comprised about one-seventh of the pulpwood output. A decrease in the number of active sawmills, from 68 in 1935 to 29 in 1962, is another noteworthy change.

There are indications that both timber supply and use have increased since 1952. Statistics for 1962, as well as subsequent data on timber use, permit us to project data as a basis for determining current trends. These data indicate, for example, that between 1953 and 1968 the volume of growing stock has gone up 22 percent — from 0.96 to 1.17 billion cubic feet, even though the area of commercial forest land has decreased slightly (from 1.63 to 1.53 million acres). Sawtimber volume has increased 16 percent.

During the period 1952-67, timber removals fluctuated sharply within short periods. Substantial year-to-year changes are possible in practically all of the elements of removals — clearings for changes in land use, reservoir and right-of-way construction, timber cut for commercial use and catastrophic losses from fires and insects. However, removals of growing stock increased 21 percent during this period. The trend for timber harvesting alone was greater — about 54 percent, or from 8.9 million to 13.7 million cubic feet. This represents an average annual increase of nearly 3 percent. The increase since 1952 reflects much heavier cutting on National Forest lands, which contributed about 85 percent of the State's cut during this period. The trend in cut from other lands has been downward.

FUTURE OPPORTUNITIES

Although in some respects South Dakota's timberlands do not measure up to those in much of the rest of the country, this does not mean that there are not big opportunities to increase supply and use. The potential growth capacity of South Dakota's forests is relatively low — only about 8 percent of the commercial forest area has a potential of more than 50 cubic feet per acre per year. This compares with roughly 45 percent for the Mountain States and 77 percent for the United States. Despite this handicap, South Dakota has some of the most intensively used and managed forest land in the United States. The State is outstanding in the West in terms of the accessibility of its timber stands and in the high level of management that has been practiced for a long time in these stands. Proximity to midwest markets of forests that are predominantly of a desirable lumber species (ponderosa pine) is a primary reason for the State's long history of good management. Still, South Dakota is utilizing considerably less than one-third of its growth potential. Therefore, it seems perfectly realistic that forestry could be accelerated in the State and the contribution of timber to the economy greatly enhanced.

Preliminary estimates indicate that 16 million cubic feet were cut from commercial forest lands in 1966. This amounted to an average of 10.4 cubic feet per acre. Although the cut per acre from commercial lands on National Forests was somewhat higher — 13.7 cubic feet — it was still slightly less than half the cut the Forest Service considered technically allowable. In other words, the supply of National Forest timber, particularly small roundwood, was more than double the volume that could be marketed.

Considerable discretion is necessary in using comparisons of cut with growth. Such

10

comparisons are not particularly useful until management and harvesting have resulted in a forest that has the age-class distribution, stocking, etc., necessary for a high level of sustained yields. Thus, while the fact that present cut is only 52 percent of growth is not particularly significant, the future relationship will be important. Growth in relation to cut must be considered in making projections and estimating potential yields. In fact, one of the assumptions used in this report to project growth, cut, and inventory to 1992 is that growth and cut of growing stock will be approximately equal at this time. On the basis of this and other assumptions,[5] projections (dash lines in chart below) indicate that by 1992 forests in the State will be yielding 40 million cubic feet from growing stock a year. Included in this is 138 million board feet of sawtimber. These yields would be equivalent to 26 cubic feet per acre including 91 board feet per acre.

Both growth and cut are expected to continue to rise beyond 1992, and the annual yield eventually could reach a level of at least 36 cubic feet per acre. This is the estimated potential from fully stocked natural stands. Yields could be higher than this if thinning and other intensive management practices are used.

The extent that timber yields increase in the years ahead depends on many factors that

[5]Assumptions used in projections are indicated as a footnote to Appendix table 28.

affect both supply and demand. Larger and more varied markets, vigorous programs of timber management and protection, and more detailed inventories are some of the important developments that are essential to minimizing the delay in realization of the State's timber potential. These factors are discussed briefly on the following pages.

Markets are a key consideration in future development. As indicated earlier, timber harvesting increased at an average annual rate of 3 percent between 1952 and 1967. Continuation at this level is essential for attaining projected yields on a sustainable basis by 1992.

A more diversified market is an important objective. Over the years, the saw log harvest for lumber has been the mainstay of South Dakota's timber economy. Although the annual harvest of saw logs is still increasing, the volume is a declining percentage of the total cut. As indicated by the chart on page 12, pulpwood and other products assumed much greater importance between 1952 and 1966. This is a significantly favorable trend. An increase in markets for small roundwood enhances opportunities to make commercial thinnings (which will accelerate growth of the remaining trees) and to utilize material that otherwise would be logging or sawmill residues.

Probably the greatest opportunities for diversifying and increasing the harvest of

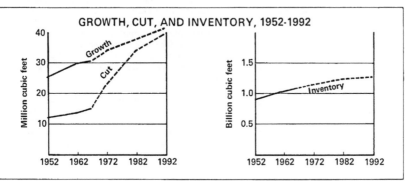

GROWTH, CUT, AND INVENTORY, 1952-1992

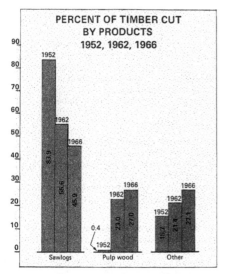

PERCENT OF TIMBER CUT
BY PRODUCTS
1952, 1962, 1966

products lie in pulpwood — and possibly veneer logs. The estimate of 54,000 cords of round pulpwood shipped to Lake States' mills in 1966 represents about 28 percent of the total output of roundwood. At least 3 times this volume could probably be harvested on a sustainable annual basis. In addition to roundwood, a substantial volume of pulp material is produced as a byproduct of sawmills — 0.8 million cubic feet (roughly 11,300 cords) of chips were shipped to Lake States' mills in 1966. Opportunities for increasing production of both roundwood and chips would be greatly enhanced if there were a closer pulpmill. The several studies that have been made of pulpwood supplies available in South Dakota and adjacent areas (Drake 1953; Fechner 1956; Chicago and North-western Railway Company 1964) indicate that the annual pulp harvest could be substantially greater than present harvests. However, these studies do not indicate that the combination of water and wood supplies is adequate for more than a small chemical mill — about 200 tons per day.

Veneer and plywood production offers another possibility for greater diversification of South Dakota's timber industry. Encouragement is lent to this possibility by the economic success in other parts of the country of peeling small logs similar to ponderosa pine logs harvested in the Black Hills. A study is currently being conducted by the Rocky Mountain. Forest and Range Experiment Station to assess plywood production and marketing opportunities and related resource requirements.

Implicit in achieving an increasing timber harvest is intensified management. Management goals necessary to provide sustainable increasing yields include attainment of a better distribution of age classes of timber stands, more commercial thinnings to improve growth, and more effective protection by earlier removal of decadent and slow growing trees susceptible to insects and disease. Other requirements include prompt success in regeneration of cut or burned areas, as well as a larger program of precommercial thinning of overstocked stands. More intensive inventories on an acre-by-acre basis are necessary to determine stand conditions with respect to stocking, age, tree quality, etc., as well as to establish priorities of cutting or other management needs.

In new inventories in western South Dakota it is especially important to obtain more useful estimates of stand stocking than are presently available. As described in the Appendix, percentage of crown closure was used in the latest survey of western South Dakota as a measure of stocking. Estimates of stocking by this technique are not sufficiently indicative of thinning and other management treatments needed to meet current objectives with respect to tree growth and product yields. Usually, stands with complete crown closure · (100 percent stocked by the crown-closure criterion) have substantially more trees per acre than desirable under good management.

Considerable differences exist among the many owners of commercial forest land with respect to technical competence and economic judgment necessary to · maximize timber yields on a sustainable basis. Owners

Ponderosa pine pulpwood is shown being loaded here for rail shipment. About 54,000 cords of roundwood and 11,300 cords of chips from sawmill residues were produced in South Dakota in 1966; the entire volume was shipped to mills in the Lake States. Commercial thinnings in ponderosa pine provide small roundwood suitable for posts as well as pulp.

Precommercial thinning of ponderosa pine such as shown at left is a common practice on the Black Hills National Forest. Gasoline-powered saws are being used by this crew. During the period 1963-67, an average of nearly 5,800 acres a year was thinned on National Forest lands in South Dakota.

of large holdings — public and private — have this competence. However, this is not true of most small private owners. Private ownership of commercial forest land amounts to 430,000 acres, or about 28 percent of the commercial forest land in the State. Of the privately owned lands, 86 percent or 368,000 acres are in the hands of farmers. Considerable technical aid has been provided small owners in the past, particularly in shelterbelt planting and utilization practices. Although some small owners do not consider timber production a primary objective in managing their forest land, many would like to substantially increase yields. What assistance is available for these owners?

Small owners can seek help from a number of sources — both private and public. Services of consulting foresters are available. Another private source is American Forest Products Industries, Inc., which offers technical advice as part of its tree farm program. In mid-1968, this organization listed 265 tree farms embracing 45,069 acres in South Dakota. Sources of public assistance include the office of the South Dakota State Forester, the Rocky Mountain Region of the Forest Service, and the Soil Conservation Service. The State Forester and U. S. D. A. Forest Service recently expanded their services by adding utilization and marketing specialists to their staffs.

14

LITERATURE CITED

Caporaso, A. P.
  1964. Forest area and timber volume in western South Dakota. U. S. Forest Serv. Res. Note INT-20, 4 pp., illus.
Chase, Clarence D.
  1967. Woodlands of eastern South Dakota. U. S. Dep. Agr., Forest Serv. North Central Forest Exp. Sta., 37 pp., (mimeo) illus.
Chicago and North Western Railway Company
  1964. A study of the wood fiber resources of the Black Hills and Wyoming tributary to the Chicago and North Western Railway. Chicago and North Western Railway Company Resources Pub. 103a. 38 pp., illus.
Drake, William, Jr.
  1953. Pulp and paper possibilities in South Dakota. South Dakota Natural Resources Comm., Pierre, South Dakota, 37 pp.
Fechner, Gilbert H.,
  1956. A survey of pulpwood resource in the northern Black Hills. U. S. Dep Agr., Forest Serv., Rocky Mountain Forest and Range Exp., Sta. Pap. 20, 21 pp., illus.
Spencer, John S., Jr., and Thomas O. Farrenkopf.
  1964. Timber products output in Colorado, Wyoming, and western South Dakota, 1962. U. S. Forest Serv. Res. Pap. INT-14, 18 pp., illus.
U. S. Forest Service.
  1958. Timber resources for America's future. Forest Resource Rep. 14, 713 pp., illus., Wash., D. C.: U. S. Govt. Printing Office.
U. S. Forest Service
  1965. Timber trends in the United States. Forest Resource Rep. 17, 235 pp., illus., Wash. D. C.: Govt. Printing Office.
Ware, E. R.
  1936. Forests of South Dakota, their economic importance and possibilities. U. S. Dep. Agr., Forest Serv., Lake States Forest Exp. Sta., St. Paul, Minn., 28 pp., illus.
Wilson, Alvin K., and John S. Spencer, Jr.
  1967. Timber resources and industries in the Rocky Mountain States. U. S. Forest Serv. Resource Bull. INT-7, 67 pp., illus.

15

APPENDIX

TERMINOLOGY[10]

Land and Forest Area

Land area. — Dry land and land temporarily or partially covered by water, such as marshes, swamps, and river flood plains; streams, sloughs, estuaries, and canals less than one-eighth of a statute mile in width; and lakes, reservoirs, and ponds less than 40 acres in area. These figures are from the U. S. Bureau of the Census, Water Area of the United States, 1960.

Forest land. — Land at least 10 percent stocked by forest trees of any size, or formerly having such tree cover, and not currently developed for nonforest use. Includes afforested areas and roadside, streamside, and shelterbelt strips of timber that have a crown width of at least 120 feet. Unimproved roads and trails, streams, and clearings within forest areas classed as forest are included if less than 120 feet in width.

Commercial forest land. — Forest land that is producing or is capable of producing crops of industrial wood and that is not withdrawn from timber utilization by statute or administrative regulation. Includes areas suitable for management to grow crops of industrial wood; such areas generally have a site quality capable of producing in excess of 20 cubic feet per acre of annual growth. This includes both accessible and inaccessible areas and both operable as well as currently inoperable areas.

Noncommercial forest land. — Unproductive forest land incapable of yielding crops of industrial wood because of adverse site conditions, and productive forest land withdrawn from commercial timber use through statute or administrative regulation.

Nonforest land. — Land that has never supported forests and lands formerly forested where forest use is precluded by development for "nonforest" uses, such as crops, improved pasture, residential areas, and city parks. Also includes improved roads and adjoining right-of-way, powerline clearings, and certain areas of water classified by the U. S. Bureau of Census as land. Includes unimproved roads, streams, canals, and nonforest strips in forest areas that are more than 120 feet wide.

Ownership Classes

National Forest lands. — Federal lands that have been designated by Executive Order or statute as National Forests.

Other federal lands. — Federal lands other than National Forests, including lands administered by the U. S. Bureau of Land Management, National Park Service, and other federal agencies. This includes lands held or managed for Indians.

State lands. — Lands owned by State or leased for more than 50 years.

Farmer-owned lands. — Lands owned by operators of farms. A farm is defined as a unit of 10 or more acres from which the sale of agricultural products totaled $50 or more annually, or a place operated as a unit of less than 10 acres from which the sale of agricultural products totaled $250 or more during the previous year.

Miscellaneous private lands. — Privately owned lands other than farmer-owned.

Forest Types

Forest land is classified into types on the basis of tree species: the type name is that of the predominant species, or group of species. Predominancy of species is based on somewhat different standards in western and east-

[10]*Definitions of some terms changed between the time of the survey of western South Dakota (1960) and that of eastern South Dakota (1965). Both definitions are shown for items where changes were most significant.*

16

ern South Dakota. In both parts of the State, cull trees as well as growing stock trees were included: (1) in western South Dakota, the predominant species is the one that has a plurality of gross cubic volume in the case of poletimber and sawtimber stands, or number of stems in sapling and seedling stands; (2) in eastern South Dakota, the predominant species is based on majority of stocking (see Stocking). Following are types that occur in the State:

Ponderosa pine. — Ponderosa pine predominates.

Oak-hickory. — This is a general type. In South Dakota, this type may be broken down into two subtypes on the basis of predominance of one or more of several species:

a. *Oak-hickory.* — Upland oaks predominate.

b. *Elm-ash-locust.* — Upland growing elm or ash, singly or in combination, predominate.

Elm-ash-cottonwood. — This is a general type. In South Dakota, this type may be broken down into four subtypes on the basis of predominance of species and topographic location (upland or lowland).

a. *Elm-ash-cottonwood.* — Predominant species are elm, ash, cottonwood, and willow, usually in combination, with occurrence on lowland sites.

b. *Cottonwood.* — Cottonwood predominates.

c. *Willow.* — Willow predominates.

d. *Lowland plains hardwoods.* — Black walnut, hackberry, bur oak, and boxelder predominate (either singly or in combination). These occur in coves or bottom lands.

White spruce. — White spruce predominates.

Pinyon-juniper. — Juniper predominates. This type is always classed as noncommercial forest.

Chaparral. — Brush and scrub hardwoods predominate; the crown canopy at maturity covers more than 50 percent of the ground. This type is always classed as noncommercial forest.

Stocking

Stocking is a measure of the degree to which growing space is effectively utilized by live trees. In the inventory of western South Dakota, stocking was determined from aerial photographs and rated on the basis of the percentage of available space occupied by tree crowns.[11] In the inventory of eastern South Dakota, stocking was rated on the basis of field measurements of number, size, and spacing of trees. When related to a stocking standard corresponding to full utilization of the growth potential of the land, these indicated the degree or percentage of stocking.

Stands have been classified as follows:

Well-stocked stands (70 percent or more stocked); medium-stocked stands (40 to 70 percent stocked); poorly stocked stands (10 to 40 percent stocked); and nonstocked area (less than 10 percent stocked).

Stand-size Classes

Sawtimber stands. — Stands at least 10 percent stocked with growing stock trees having (1) in western South Dakota, a minimum net volume per acre of 1,500 board feet (International ¼-inch rule) in sawtimber trees; (2) in eastern South Dakota, one-half or more of the total stocking in sawtimber and poletimber trees and with sawtimber stocking at least equal to poletimber stocking.

Old-growth sawtimber. — A sawtimber stand in which the majority of the net board-foot volume is in sawtimber trees 21.0 inches d.b.h. and larger.

Young-growth sawtimber. — A sawtimber stand in which the majority of the net board-foot volume is in sawtimber trees less than 20.9 inches d.b.h.

Poletimber stands. — Stands that (1) are at least 10 percent stocked with growing stock trees; (2) fail to meet sawtimber stand specifications; and (3) have at least one-half the

---

[11] *Although used to rate stocking in western South Dakota, percentage of available space occupied by tree crowns is not generally considered a reliable indication of the need for thinning and other management measures.*

total stocking in poletimber and larger trees and with poletimber stocking exceeding that of sawtimber.

Sapling-seedling stands. — Stands that (1) are at least 10 percent stocked with growing stock trees; (2) fail to meet sawtimber or poletimber stand specifications; and (3) have more than one-half of the total stocking in sapling and/or seedlings.

Nonstocked stands. — Commercial forest land less than 10 percent stocked with growing stock trees.

Site Classes

A classification of forest land in terms of inherent capacity to grow crops of industrial wood in fully stocked natural stands.

Tree Classification

Growing stock trees. — Sawtimber trees, poletimber trees, saplings and seedlings; i.e., all live trees except rough and rotten trees.

Sawtimber trees. — Live trees of commercial species containing at least one log (10-foot in western South Dakota and 12-foot in eastern South Dakota). Softwoods must be at least 9.0 inches d.b.h. and hardwoods at least 11.0 inches d.b.h. Maximum permissible cull is two-thirds of the board-foot volume.

Poletimber trees. — Live trees of commercial species at least 5.0 inches d.b.h. but smaller than sawtimber size and of good form and vigor.

Sapling and seedling trees. — Live trees of commercial species less than 5.0 inches d.b.h. and having form and quality to qualify as potential poletimber trees.

Rotten trees. — Live trees of commercial species that will not now or in the future qualify as sawtimber trees because of dimensions — diameter and minimum size specifications for saw logs and/or will not meet sawtimber tree requirements because of excessive defect, primarily due to rot; i.e., when more than 50 percent of the cull volume is attributable to rot.

Rough trees. — Live trees of (1) commercial species that will not now or in the future qualify as sawtimber trees because of dimensions — diameter and minimum size specifications for saw logs and/or will not meet sawtimber tree requirements because of excessive defect, primarily due to roughness or poor form; and (2) noncommercial species.

Timber Volumes

Growing stock volume. — Net cubic-foot volume of sawtimber trees and poletimber trees above 1-foot stump to a minimum 4.0-inch top (outside bark) or to the point where the central stem breaks into limbs.

Sawtimber volume. — Net volume in board feet (International ¼-inch rule) of the saw log portion of live sawtimber trees. The volume of sawtimber is included in the volume of growing stock.

Saw log portion. — That portion of the bole of sawtimber trees between the stump and the merchantable top. The latter varies from 5 to 10 inches inside bark depending on d.b.h. and whether trees are softwoods or hardwoods.

Upper stem portion. — That portion of the bole of sawtimber trees above the merchantable top to a minimum top diameter of 4.0 inches (outside bark) or to the point where the central stem breaks into limbs.

Log grade. — Sawtimber volume is classified as to quality on the basis of log grades. The grades are defined by external log features, principally by the occurrence and characteristics of knots. Hardwoods are classified into four grades in accordance with "Hardwood Log Grade for Standard Lumber" issued by the Forest Products Laboratory under the designation D1737 in 1953 and standards for hardwood tie and timber logs. Softwood logs are classified into four grades, which are defined as follows:

Grade 1 (select logs) are essentially smooth and surface clear, except that in logs 16 inches and larger in diameter a few visible knots are permitted, provided there are no more than one large knot, or two medium or small knots, or four pin knots.

18

Knot sizes for all grades are:

Pin knots (0.5 inch or less)

Small knots (0.5 to 0.75 inch)

Medium knots (0.75 to 1.5 inches)

Large knots (Larger than 1.5 inches)

Occasional logs having a greater number of knots are admitted provided these knots may be boxed in an area not exceeding one-third the area of one face or an equivalent area of two faces.

Grade 2 (shop logs) display relatively few knots of any size, which are so spaced that at least 50 percent of the surface of the log is in smooth, clear areas, the size of which must be at least one-fourth the girth of the log in width by 4 feet or more in length.

A log with no more than 12 medium or smaller knots, or more than eight large ones, may immediately be classed as grade 2. If this number of knots is exceeded, the clear area basis governs.

Grade 3 (common logs) display either (a) pin, small, or medium knots of which 80 percent are either live or will cut out red (intergrown) beneath the slab, or (2) 16 dead knots (an average of four per face) averaging medium in size.

Grade 4 (low common logs) display medium, large, and very large live and/or dead knots in excess of the numbers permitted in grades 2 and 3.

Growth and Mortality

Net annual growth of sawtimber or growing stock. — The annual change in board-foot volume of sawtimber and of cubic-foot volume of sawtimber and poletimber combined. Net annual growth is the resultant of increment in net volume on trees that survived through the period over which annual growth was averaged, plus the ingrowth volume, minus the volume of trees that either died or became cull during the period.

Mortality of sawtimber or growing stock. — The net board-foot volume of sound wood in live sawtimber trees and net cubic-foot volume of sawtimber and poletimber trees combined that die annually from natural causes. These causes include fire, insects, disease, other, and unknown. The "other" category includes death due to animals (other than man), weather, and suppression. Death caused by logging or other activities of man is not included.

Removals

Total removals from growing stock and sawtimber. — The net cubic-foot and board-foot volume in growing stock and sawtimber trees, respectively, that was removed from the inventory by harvesting including logging residues; by cultural operations, such as timber stand improvement, land clearing; or by changes in land use.

Timber products. — Roundwood products and plant byproducts. Roundwood products include material cut from growing stock on commercial forest land; from other sources, such as cull trees, salvable dead trees, limbs, and saplings; and from trees on noncommercial and nonforest lands.

Roundwood products. — Logs, poles, posts, bolts, or other round sections cut from trees for industrial or consumer uses.

Logging residues. — The unused portions of trees cut or killed by logging.

Plant byproducts. — Wood products, such as pulp chips and lathe, obtained incidental to manufacture of primary products.

Plant residues. — Wood materials from manufacturing plants not utilized for some product. Includes slabs, edgings, trimmings, miscuts, sawdust, and shavings.

19

Tree Species

The following includes both the principal species as well as some that are uncommon. Not all species were encountered on inventory sample plots.

Softwoods

Ponderosa pine	*Pinus ponderosa*
Redcedar	*Juniperus virginiana*
Western juniper	*J. occidentalis*
White spruce	*Picea glauca* var. *densata*

Hardwoods

Select white oaks	
Bur oak	*Quercus macrocarpa*
Chinkapin oak	*Q. muehlenbergii*
White oak	*Q. alba*
Select red oaks	
Northern red oak	*Quercus rubra*
Shumard oak	*Q. Shumardii*
Other white oaks	
Post oak	*Quercus stellata* var. *stellata*
Other red oaks	
Black oak	*Quercus velutina*
Pin oak	*Q. palustris*
Shingle oak	*Q. imbricaria*
Hickory	
Bitternut hickory	*Carya cordiformis*
Mockernut hickory	*C. tomentosa*
Pecan	*C. illinoensis*
Pignut hickory	*C. glabra*
Shagbark hickory	*C. ovata*
Shellbark hickory	*C. laciniosa*
Hard maple	
Black maple	*Acer nigrum*
Sugar maple	*A. saccharum*
Soft maple	
Boxelder	*Acer negundo*
Red maple	*A. rubrum* var. *rubrum*
Silver maple	*A. saccharinum*
Ash	
Green ash	*Fraxinus pennsylvanica*
Cottonwood	*Populus deltoides*
Basswood	
American basswood	*Tilia americana*
Black walnut	*Jaglans nigra*
Other eastern hardwoods	
American elm	*Ulmus americana*
Rock elm	*U. thomasii*
Siberian elm	*U. pumila*

Slippery elm	*U. rubra*
Hackberry	*Celtis occidentalis*
Sycamore	*Platanus occidentalis*
Black willow	*Salix nigra*
Black cherry	*Prunus serotina*
Other soft hardwoods	
Kentucky coffeetree	*Gymnocladus dioicus*
Northern catalpa	*Catalpa speciosa*
Ohio buckeye	*Aesculus glabra*
Quaking aspen	*Populus tremuloides*
Red mulberry	*Morus rubra*
River birch	*Betula nigra*
White mulberry	*Morus alba*
Other hard hardwoods	
Black locust	*Robinia pseudoacacia*
Common persimmon	*Diospyros virginiana*
Flowering dogwood	*Cornus florida*
Honey locust	*Gleditsia triacanthos*

20

SURVEY METHODS
AND RELIABILITY OF DATA

Interpretation of aerial photographs, together with sample measurements of trees on the ground, provided the principal source of statistics on acreage, volume, growth, and mortality in South Dakota. Although this general approach was used throughout the State, the evolution in many techniques between the time of the western South Dakota inventory (1960) and that of the eastern portion of the State (1965) resulted in certain significant differences in detailed methods.

Even within western South Dakota, methods varied. All lands were type-mapped within the boundaries of the Black Hills National Forest by the use of aerial photographs. These maps provided a basis for estimating acreage by ownerships, land classes, forest types, etc. Trees were measured and classified on 137 locations on National Forest lands within the Black Hills National Forest. These locations, which had originally been established in 1953-54, were remeasured to estimate volume, growth, and mortality. Each location consisted of a cluster of from one to four rectangular plots within each of which sample size varied with size and type of trees; sawtimber trees for example were measured on a 1/5-acre area. Standard measurements and classifications were made of tree diameters, heights, species, etc.

Lands in western South Dakota outside the Black Hills National Forest were not mapped but were sampled using a systematic grid of points on aerial photographs to estimate acreages. A large number of points was examined to classify forest and nonforest lands and to distinguish commercial forest from noncommercial forest. The 874 points classified as commercial forest were further interpreted for timber type, stand-size class, etc. From these 874 points, 30 were selected at random as locations for field measurements. These 30 locations were established

and measured in the same manner as those on the Black Hills National Forest.

Eastern South Dakota was sampled on photos using 323,141 well-distributed points. A subsample proportional to area represented by these points was checked at 217 forest and 80,336 nonforest locations. On each of the 217 forest locations, detailed tree measurements and classifications were made within a 1-acre area.

Estimates of timber removals are based on various sources of information. Volumes of timber products and mill residues were obtained from canvasses of almost all wood processing plants. These canvasses provided 1962 information for western South Dakota and 1964 information for eastern South Dakota. Other removals resulting from changes in land use, thinnings, etc., could not be determined by surveys, but were estimated on the basis of the best available information.

Forest resource statistics are subject to both human and sampling errors. The amount of human error cannot be measured, but is minimized through close supervision and adequate training of employees, and through rechecking of all phases of the work. Sampling errors are subject to the laws of chance and may be estimated by statistical methods. These errors are held to acceptable levels by adjusting the survey design and sample size. Chances are two out of three that the actual area of commercial forest is within ±1.16 percent of the estimated area (1,533,900 acres). Included in this estimated area are the 1,098,000 acres within the boundaries of the Black Hills National Forest which, because it was completely mapped, is considered free of sampling error.

The sampling error for growing stock volume (1,085 million cubic feet) is estimated at ±5.19 percent, and for timber cut during harvest (13,289,000 cubic feet) at ±3.2 percent.

TIMBER STATISTICS

Table 1.--<u>Area by land classes, South Dakota, 1962</u>

Land class	Thousand acres
Forest land:	
Commercial	1,534
Productive reserved	19
Unproductive	180
Total forest	1,733
Nonforest land:	
Cropland[1]	17,424
Pasture and range	26,584
Other[2]	3,141
Total nonforest	47,149
Total area[3]	48,882

[1] Source: 1959 Census of Agriculture.
[2] Includes swampland, industrial urban areas, other nonforest land, and land (366,000 acres) classed as water by Forest Survey standards, but defined as water by the U.S. Bureau of Census as land.
[3] Source: U.S. Bureau of the Census, Land and Water Area of the United States, 1960.

Table 2.--<u>Area of commercial forest land, by ownership classes, South Dakota, 1962</u>

Ownership class	Thousand acres
National Forest	957
Other Federal:	
Bureau of Land Management	7
Indian	66
Miscellaneous Federal	9
Total other Federal	82
State	65
County and municipal	--
Forest industry[1]	--
Farmer-owned	368
Miscellaneous private:	62
Individual[2]	--
Corporate[2]	--
Total miscellaneous private	62
All ownerships	1,534

[1] Forest industry has been combined with miscellaneous private to avoid disclosure of holdings of an individual owner.
[2] Not available.

22

Table 3.--Area of commercial forest land, by stand size and ownership classes, South Dakota, 1962

(Thousand acres)

Stand size class	All ownerships	National Forest	Other public	Forest industry[1]	Farmer and miscellaneous private
Sawtimber stands:[2]					
Old growth	(3/)	--	--	--	(3/)
Young growth	813	569	70	--	174
Total sawtimber	813	569	70	--	174
Poletimber stands	637	343	71	--	223
Sapling and seedling stands	65	33	6	--	26
Nonstocked areas	19	12	(3/)	--	7
All classes	1,534	957	147	--	430

[1] Forest industry has been combined with farmer and miscellaneous private to avoid disclosure of holdings of an individual owner.
[2] Breakdown by old and young growth required only in the West; all sawtimber stands in the East are included in young growth.
[3] Less than 0.5 thousand acres.

Table 4.--Area of commercial forest land, by stand-volume and ownership classes, South Dakota, 1962

(Thousand acres)

Stand volume per acre[1]	All ownerships	National Forest	Other public	Forest industry[2]	Farmer and miscellaneous private
Less than 1,500 board feet	751	387	86	--	278
1,500 to 5,000 board feet	714	511	61	--	142
More than 5,000 board feet	69	59	--	--	10
All classes	1,534	957	147	--	430

[1] International ¼-inch rule.
[2] Forest industry has been combined with farmer and miscellaneous private to avoid disclosure of holdings of an individual owner.

23

Table 5.--Area of commercial forest land, by stocking classes of all live trees, and by stand-size classes, South Dakota, 1962

(Thousand acres)

Stocking class	All stands	Sawtimber stands	Poletimber stands	Sapling and seedling stands	Non-stocked stands
70 percent or more	220	127	86	7	
40 to 70 percent	1,080	602	452	26	
10 to 40 percent	215	84	99	32	--
Less than 10 percent	19	--	--	--	19
All classes	1,534	813	637	65	19

Table 6.--Area of commercial forest land, by site and ownership classes, South Dakota, 1962

(Thousand acres)

Site class	All ownerships	National Forest	Other public	Forest industry[1]	Farmer and miscellaneous private
50 to 85 cu. ft.	116	63	12	--	41
20 to 50 cu. ft.	1,418	894	135	--	389
All classes	1,534	957	147	--	430

[1] Forest industry has been combined with farmer and miscellaneous private to avoid disclosure of holdings of an individual owner.

24

Table 7.--Area of commercial forest land, by forest
types and ownership classes, South Dakota, 1962

(Thousand acres)

Forest type	All ownerships	Public ownerships	Private ownerships
Softwoods:			
Ponderosa pine	1,330	1,047	283
White spruce	23	21	2
Total softwood types	1,353	1,068	285
Hardwoods:			
Oak-hickory	8	4	4
Elm-ash-locust	36	2	34
Willow	7	1	6
Lowland plains hardwoods	23	2	21
Elm-ash-cottonwood	64	21	43
Cottonwood	43	6	37
Total hardwood types	181	36	145
All types	1,534	1,104	430

Table 8.--Area of noncommercial forest land,
by forest types, South Dakota, 1962

(Thousand acres)

Type	All areas	Productive reserved areas	Unproductive areas
Ponderosa pine	22	19	3
White spruce	(1/)	(1/)	--
Lowland plains mixed hardwoods	6	--	6
Elm-ash-cottonwood	20	--	20
Cottonwood	3		3
Other hardwoods (unclassified)	71		71
Chaparral	3	--	3
Pinyon-juniper	74	--	74
All types	199	19	180

1/ Less than 0.5 thousand acres.

25

Table 9.—Number of growing stock trees on commercial forest land, by species and diameter classes, South Dakota, 1962

(Thousand trees)

Species	All classes	Diameter class (inches at breast height)											
		1.0-2.9	3.0-4.9	5.0-6.9	7.0-8.9	9.0-10.9	11.0-12.9	13.0-14.9	15.0-16.9	17.0-18.9	19.0-20.9	21.0-28.9	29.0 and larger
Softwoods:													
Ponderosa pine	502,906	217,592	98,980	86,438	49,134	22,957	13,357	7,582	3,649	1,784	919	512	2
White spruce	8,528	2,020	1,837	1,864	1,018	443	428	424	219	96	87	92	--
Cedar	42	42	--	--	--	--	--	--	--	--	--	--	--
Total softwoods	511,476	219,654	100,817	88,302	50,152	23,400	13,785	8,006	3,868	1,880	1,006	604	2
Hardwoods:													
Bur oak	72	151	462	536	336	137	108	26	10	3	3	--	--
Hard maple	82	--	--	67	--	15	--	--	--	--	--	--	--
Ash	8,312	2,208	1,896	2,320	767	502	297	207	74	20	12	9	--
Black Walnut	131	126	--	--	--	--	--	--	--	--	3	2	--
Elm	3,801	625	598	983	566	292	301	202	99	48	32	44	11
Hackberry	347	15	210	61	38	17	6	--	--	12	3	--	--
Soft maple	214	103	--	--	31	40	18	8	--	--	2	--	--
Basswood	624	160	--	104	154	140	30	19	12	12	5	--	--
Cottonwood	4,127	897	810	1,199	402	221	160	128	79	72	60	76	23
Willow	837	612	--	29	121	17	30	13	6	5	2	2	--
Other soft hdwds.	881	498	105	35	59	113	37	18	11	--	3	2	--
Other hardwoods	1,679	138	108	951	301	181	--	--	--	--	--	--	--
Other white oak	252	189	63	--	--	--	--	--	--	--	--	--	--
Black cherry	130	130	--	--	--	--	--	--	--	--	--	--	--
Total hardwoods	23,189	5,852	4,252	6,285	2,775	1,494	1,168	621	291	160	122	135	34
All species	534,665	225,506	105,069	94,587	52,927	24,894	14,953	8,627	4,159	2,040	1,128	739	36

26

Table 10.--Net volume of timber on commerical forest land, by class
of timber, and softwoods and hardwoods, South Dakota, 1962

(Million cubic feet)

Class of timber	All species	Softwoods	Hardwoods
Sawtimber trees:			
Saw-log portion	666	626	40
Upper-stem portion	74	67	7
Total sawtimber	740	693	47
Poletimber trees	345	314	31
All growing-stock trees	1,085	1,007	78
Rough trees	10	1	9
Rotten trees	21	3	18
Salvable dead trees	6	6	--
Total, all timber	1,122	1,017	105

Table 11.--Net volume of growing stock and sawtimber on commercial forest land,
by ownership classes, and softwoods and hardwoods, South Dakota, 1962

Ownership class	Growing stock (Million cubic feet)			Sawtimber (Million board feet)[1]		
	All species	Softwoods	Hardwoods	All species	Softwoods	Hardwoods
National Forest	781	781	(2/)	2,687	2,687'	(3/)
Other public	76	62	14	253	219	34
Farmer and miscel- laneous private[4]	228	164	64	776	563	213
All ownerships	1,085	1,007	78	3,716	3,469	247

[1] International ¼-inch rule.
[2] Less than 0.5 million cubic feet.
[3] Less than 0.5 million board feet.
[4] Forest industry has been combined with farmer and miscellaneous private
to avoid disclosure of holdings of an individual owner.

27

Table 12.--Net volume of growing stock on commercial forest land,
by species and diameter classes, South Dakota, 1962

(Million cubic feet)

Species	Diameter class (inches at breast height)										
	All classes	5.0-6.9	7.0-8.9	9.0-10.9	11.0-12.9	13.0-14.9	15.0-16.9	17.0-18.9	19.0-20.9	21.0-28.9	29.0 and larger
Softwoods:											
Ponderosa pine	961	127	179	151	158	127	88	57	40	34	(1/)
White spruce	46	3	5.	4	6	9	7	3	3	6	--
Total softwoods	1,007	130	184	155	164	136	95	60	43	40	(1/)
Hardwoods:											
Bur oak	4	1	1	1	1	(1/)	(1/)	(1/)	(1/)	--	--
Hard maple	(1/)	(1/)	--	(1/)	--	--	--	--	--	--	--
Ash	19	4	3	3	3	3	2	1	(1/)	(1/)	--
Black walnut	(1/)	--	--	--	--	--	--	--	(1/)	(1/)	--
Elm	16	1	1	2	3	2	2	1	1	2	1
Hackberry	(1/)	(1/)	(1/)	(1/)	(1/)	--	--	--	--	--	--
Soft maple	1	--	(1/)	(1/)	(1/)	(1/)	--	1	(1/)	--	--
Basswood	2	(1/)	1	1	(1/)	(1/)	(1/)	--	(1/)	--	--
Cottonwood	28	3	2	2	3	3	2	2	3	6	2
Willow	1	(1/)	1	(1/)	(1/)	(1/)	(1/)	(1/)	(1/)	(1/)	--
Other hardwoods	7	2	1	1	2	1	(1/)	--	(1/)	(1/)	--
Total hardwoods	78	11	10	10	12	9	6	5	4	8	3
All species	1,085	141	194	165	176	145	101	65	47	.48	3

1/ Less than 0.5 million cubic feet.

28

Table 13.--Net volume of sawtimber on commercial forest land,
by species and diameter classes, South Dakota, 1962

(Million board feet)[1]

Species	Diameter class (inches at breast height)								
	All classes	9.0-10.9[2]	11.0-12.9	13.0-14.9	15.0-16.9	17.0-18.9	19.0-20.9	21.0-28.9	29.0 and larger
Softwoods:									
Ponderosa pine	3,268	748	752	608	456	300	217	185	2
White spruce	201	26	33	44	34	16	15	33	--
Total softwoods	3,469	774	785	652	490	316	232	218	2
Hardwoods:									
Bur oak	6	--	3	1	1	(3/)	1	--	--
Ash	40	--	12	14	7	3	2	2	--
Black walnut	1	--	--	--	--	--	(3/)	1	--
Elm	58	--	11	11	9	7	6	11	3
Hackberry	(3/)	--	(3/)	--	--	--	--	--	--
Soft maple	3	--	(3/)	1	--	1	1	--	--
Basswood	1	--	1	(3/)	(3/)	--	(3/)	--	--
Cottonwood	120	--	14	15	11	14	14	38	14
Willow	7	--	2	1	1	1	(3/)	2	--
Other hardwoods	11	--	9	1	1	--	(3/)	(3/)	--
Total hardwoods	247	--	52	44	30	26	24	54	17
All species	3,716	774	837	696	520	342	256	272	19

[1] International ¼-inch rule.

[2] Softwoods only.

[3] Less than 0.5 million board feet.

Table 14.--Net volume of sawtimber on commercial forest land, by species and log grades, South Dakota, 1962

(Million board feet)[1]

Species	All grades	Log grade			
		1	2	3	4
Softwoods:					
Ponderosa pine	3,268	66	150	344	2,708
White spruce[2]	201	4	9	21	167
Total softwoods	3,469	70	159	365	2,875
Hardwoods:					
Bur oak	6	--	(3/)	5	1
Ash	40	1	8	21	10
Black walnut	1	1	(3/)	(3/)	--
Elm	58	10	13	25	10
Hackberry	(3/)	(3/)	(3/)	(3/)	(3/)
Soft maple	3	1	(3/)	1	1
Basswood	1	(3/)	1	(3/)	(3/)
Cottonwood	120	29	13	70	8
Willow	7	--	(3/)	5	2
Other hardwoods	11	--	2	6	3
Total hardwoods	247	42	37	133	35
All species	3,716	112	196	498	2,910

[1] International ¼-inch rule.

[2] Spruce not graded but volume has been apportioned among grade classes on the basis of ponderosa pine.

[3] Less than 0.5 million board feet.

.30

Table 15.--Volume of growing stock and sawtimber on commercial forest
land, by stand-size classes and by softwoods and hardwoods,
South Dakota, 1962

Stand-size class	All species	Softwoods	Hardwoods
	GROWING STOCK (Million cubic feet)		
Sawtimber stands	776	729	47
Poletimber stands	304	274	30
Sapling and seedling stands	4	3	1
Nonstocked areas	1	1	(1/)
All classes	1,085	1,007	78
	SAWTIMBER (Million board feet)$\frac{2}{}$		
Sawtimber stands	3,122	2,917	205
Poletimber stands	578	540	38
Sapling and seedling stands	12	8	4
Nonstocked areas	4	4	(1/)
All classes	3,716	3,469	247

$\frac{1}{}$ Less than 0.5 million feet
$\frac{2}{}$ International ¼-inch rule

31

Table 16.--Net annual growth[1] and removals[2] of growing stock on commercial forest land, by species, South Dakota, 1962

(Thousand cubic feet)

Species	Net annual growth	Annual timber removals
Softwoods:		
Ponderosa pine	25,880	12,066
White spruce	1,075	1
Total softwoods	26,955	12,067
Hardwoods:		
Bur oak	190	233
Hard maple	20	0
Ash	650	237
Elm	460	72
Hackberry	40	0
Soft maple	50	0
Basswood	140	0
Cottonwood	1,670	707
Willow	110	11
Other hardwoods	169	2
Total hardwoods	3,499	1,262
All species	30,454	13,329

[1] Average net annual growth for the last decade estimated to be 29,594,000 cubic feet.
[2] Average annual timber removals for the last decade estimated to be 13,245,000 cubic feet.

Table 17.--Net annual growth[1] and removals[2] of growing stock on commercial forest land, by ownership classes, and softwoods and hardwoods, South Dakota, 1962

(Thousand cubic feet)

Ownership class	Net annual growth			Annual timber removals		
	All species	Softwoods	Hardwoods	All species	Softwoods	Hardwoods
National Forest	20,086	20,083	3	10,978	10,978	0
Other public	2,592	1,975	617	232	114	118
Farmer and miscellaneous private[3]	7,776	4,897	2,879	2,119	975	1,144
All ownerships	30,454	26,955	3,499	13,329	12,067	1,262

[1] Average net annual growth for the last decade estimated to be 29,594,000 cubic feet.
[2] Average annual timber removals for the last decade estimated to be 13,245,000 cubic feet.
[3] Forest industry has been combined with farmer and miscellaneous private to avoid disclosure of holdings of an individual owner.

32

Table 18.--Net annual growth[1] and removals[2] of sawtimber
on commercial forest land, by species, South Dakota, 1962

(Thousand board feet)[3]

Species	Net annual growth	Annual timber removals
Softwoods:		
Ponderosa pine	86,460	53,257
White spruce	4,598	5
Total softwoods	91,058	53,262
Hardwoods:		
Bur oak	660	619
Ash	2,410	600
Elm	2,050	204
Hackberry	40	0
Soft maple	350	0
Basswood	120	0
Cottonwood	5,400	3,841
Willow	380	25
Other hardwoods	379	17
Total hardwoods	11,789	5,306
All species	102,847	58,568

[1]Average net annual growth for the last decade
estimated to be 101,087,000 board feet.
[2]Average annual timber removals for the last decade
estimated to be 56,475,000 board feet.
[3]International ¼-inch rule.

Table 19.--Net annual growth[1] and removals[2] of sawtimber on commercial forest
land, by ownership classes, and softwoods and hardwoods, South Dakota, 1962

(Thousand board feet)[3]

Ownership class	Net annual growth			Annual timber removals		
	All species	Softwoods	Hardwoods	All species	Softwoods	Hardwoods
National Forest	67,988	67,986	2	49,065	49,065	0
Other public	8,919	7,155	1,764	661	412	249
Farmer and miscellaneous private[4]	25,940	15,917	10,023	8,842	3,785	5,057
All ownerships	102,847	91,058	11,789	58,568	53,262	5,306

[1]Average net annual growth for the last decade estimated to be 101,087,000
board feet.
[2]Average annual timber removals for the last decade estimated to be
56,475,000 board feet.
[3]International ¼-inch rule.
[4]Forest industry has been combined with farmer and miscellaneous private
to avoid disclosure of holdings of an individual owner.

33

Table 20. --Mortality[1] of growing stock and sawtimber on commercial
forest land, by species, South Dakota, 1962

Species	Growing stock	Sawtimber
	Thousand cubic feet	Thousand board feet[2]
Softwoods:		
Ponderosa pine	1,214	4,251
White spruce	251	1,308
Total softwoods	1,465	5,559
Hardwoods:		
Bur oak	10	--
Ash	330	290
Elm	60	90
Cottonwood	240	80
Other hardwoods	71	155
Total hardwoods	711	615
All species	2,176	6,174

[1] Average annual mortality for the last decade estimated to
be 3,036,000 cubic feet and 7,934,000 board feet.
[2] International ¼-inch rule.

Table 21.--Mortality[1] of growing stock and sawtimber on commercial forest land,
by ownership classes, and softwoods and hardwoods, South Dakota, 1962

Ownership class	Growing stock (Thousand cubic feet)			Sawtimber (Thousand board feet)[2]		
	All species	Softwoods	Hardwoods	All species	Softwoods	Hardwoods
National Forest	1,218	1,218	(3/)	4,476	4,474	°
Other public	208	66	142	394	306	88
Farmer and miscellaneous private[4]	750	181	569	1,304	779	525
All ownerships	2,176	1,465	711	6,174	5,559	615

[1] Average annual mortality for the last decade estimated to be 3,036,000
cubic feet and 7,934,000 board feet.
[2] International ¼-inch rule.
[3] Less than 0.5 thousand cubic feet.
[4] Forest industry has been combined with farmer and miscellaneous private
to avoid disclosure of holdings of an individual owner.

Table 22.--Mortality[1] of growing stock and sawtimber on commercial forest land, by causes, and softwoods and hardwoods, South Dakota, 1962

Cause	Growing stock (Thousand cubic feet)			Sawtimber (Thousand board feet)[2]		
	All species	Softwoods	Hardwoods	All species	Softwoods	Hardwoods
Fire	--	--	--	--	--	--
Insects	343	343	--	1,528	1,528	--
Disease	1,228	827	401	3,526	3,141	385
Other and unknown	605	295	310	1,120	890	230
All causes	2,176	1,465	711	6,174	5,559	615

[1] Average annual mortality for the last decade estimated to be 3,036,000 cubic feet and 7,934,000 board feet.
[2] International ¼-inch rule.

Table 23.--Output of timber products, by source of material and softwoods and hardwoods, South Dakota, 1962

Product and species group	Standard units	Total output		Roundwood products		Plant byproducts	
		Number of units	Thousand cubic feet	Number of units	Thousand cubic feet	Number of units	Thousand cubic feet
Saw logs:							
Softwood	M bd. ft.[1]	38,958	6,493	38,958	6,493	0	0
Hardwood	M bd. ft.[1]	1,200	165	1,200	165	0	0
Total	M bd. ft.[1]	40,158	6,658	40,158	6,658	0	0
Veneer logs and bolts:							
Softwood	M bd. ft.[1]	0	0	0	0	0	0
Hardwood	M bd. ft.[1]	1,532	199	1,532	199	0	0
Total	M bd. ft.[1]	1,532	199	1,532	199	0	0
Pulpwood:							
Softwood	Std. cords[2]	41,000	3,564	34,000	3,060	7,000	504
Hardwood	Std. cords[2]	0	0	0	0	0	0
Total	Std. cords[2]	41,000	3,564	34,000	3,060	7,000	504
Cooperage:							
Softwood	M bd. ft.[1]	0	0	0	0	0	0
Hardwood	M bd. ft.[1]	0	0	0	0	0	0
Total	M bd. ft.[1]	0	0	0	0	0	0
Piling:							
Softwood	M linear ft.	12	10	12	10	0	0
Hardwood	M linear ft.	0	0	0	0	0	0
Total	M linear ft.	12	10	12	10	0	0
Poles:							
Softwood	M pieces	92	545	92	545	0	0
Hardwood	M pieces	6	25	6	25	0	0
Total	M pieces	98	570	98	570	0	0

(con. next page)

Table 23 (con.)

Product and species group	Standard units	Total output Number of units	Total output Thousand cubic feet	Roundwood products Number of units	Roundwood products Thousand cubic feet	Plant byproducts Number of units	Plant byproducts Thousand cubic feet
Mine timbers (Round):							
Softwood	M cu. ft.	0	0	0	0	0	0
Hardwood	M cu. ft.	0	0	0	0	0	0
Total	M cu. ft.	0	0	0	0	0	0
Posts (Round and split):							
Softwood	M pieces	746	754	746	754	0	0
Hardwood	M pieces	100	79	100	79	0	0
Total	M pieces	846	833	846	833	0	0
Other:[3]							
Softwood	M cu. ft.	447	447	447	447	0	0
Hardwood	M cu. ft.	158	158	125	125	33	33
Total	M cu. ft.	605	605	572	572	33	33
Total industrial products:							
Softwood			11,813		11,309		504
Hardwood			626		593		33
Total			12,439		11,902		537
Fuelwood:							
Softwood	Std. cords	7,931	528	6,931	456	1,000	72
Hardwood	Std. cords	24,500	1,513	23,124	1,428	1,376	85
Total	Std. cords	32,431	2,041	30,055	1,884	2,376	157
All products:							
Softwood			12,341		11,765		576
Hardwood			2,139		2,021		118
Total			14,480		13,786		694

[1] International ¼-inch rule.
[2] Rough-wood basis (includes chips converted to equivalent standard cords).
[3] Mostly miscellaneous farm timbers.

36

Table 24.--Output of roundwood products by source, and softwoods and hardwoods, South Dakota, 1962

(Thousand cubic feet)

Product and species group	All :sources:	Growing stock trees[1]			Rough and :rotten :trees[1]/	Salvable dead trees[1]/	Other :sources[2]/
		Total	Sawtimber	Poletimber			
Industrial products:							
Saw logs:							
Softwood	6,493	6,428	6,428	0	0	65	0
Hardwood	165	163	163	0	1	0	1
Total	6,658	6,591	6.591	0	1	65	1
Veneer logs and bolts:							
Softwood	0	0	0	0	0	0	0
Hardwood	199	199	199	0	0	0	0
Total	199	199	199	0	0	0	0
Pulpwood:							
Softwood	3,060	3,060	918	2,142	0	0	0
Hardwood	0	0	0	0	0	0	0
Total	3,060	3,060	918	2,142	0	0	0
Miscellaneous industrial products:							
Cooperage:							
Softwood	0	0	0	0	0	0	0
Hardwood	0	0	0	0	0	0	0
Total	0	0	0	0	0	0	0
Piling:							
Softwood	10	10	10	0	0	0	0
Hardwood	0	0	0	0	0	0	0
Total	10	10	10	0	0	0	0
Poles:							
Softwood	545	512	508	4	1	32	0
Hardwood	25	23	7	16	2	0	0
Total	570	535	515	20	3	32	0
Mine timbers (Round):							
Softwood	0	0	0	0	0	0	0
Hardwood	0	0	0	0	0	0	0
Total	0	0	0	0	0	0	0
Posts (Round and split):							
Softwood	754	729	541	188	0	0	25
Hardwood	79	34	2	32	0	0	45
Total	833	763	543	220	0	0	70
Other:							
Softwood	447	402	402	0	0	45	0
Hardwood	125	125	75	50	0	0	0
Total	572	527	477	50	0	45	0
All miscellaneous industrial products:							
Softwood	1,756	1,653	1,461	192	1	77	25
Hardwood	229	182	84	93	2	0	45
Total	1,985	1,835	1,545	290	3	77	70
All industrial products:							
Softwood	11,309	11,141	8,807	2,334	1	142	25
Hardwood	593	544	446	98	3	0	46
Total	11,902	11,685	9,253	2,432	4	142	71

(con. next page)

37

Table 24 (con.)

Product and species group	All sources	Growing stock trees[1]			Rough and rotten trees[1]	Salvable dead trees[1]	Other sources[2]
		Total	Sawtimber	Poletimber			
Fuelwood:							
Softwood	456	189	104	85	91	38	138
Hardwood	1,428	638	352	286	308	21	461
Total	1,884	827	456	371	399	59	599
All products:							
Softwood	11,765	11,330	8,911	2,419	92	180	163
Hardwood	2,021	1,182	798	384	311	21	507
Total	13,786	12,512	9,709	2,803	403	201	670

[1] On commercial forest land.
[2] Includes trees less than 5.0 inches in diameter, treetops and limbs from commercial forest areas or material from noncommercial forest land or nonforest land such as fence rows or suburban areas.

Table 25.--Timber removals[1] from growing stock on commercial forest land, by items, and softwoods and hardwoods, South Dakota, 1962

(Thousand cubic feet)

Item	All species	Softwoods	Hardwoods
Roundwood products:			
Saw logs	6,591	6,428	163
Veneer logs and bolts	199	0	199
Pulpwood	3,060	3,060	0
Cooperage logs and bolts	0	0	0
Piling	10	10	0
Poles	535	512	23
Mine timbers	0	0	0
Posts	763	729	34
Other	527	402	125
Fuelwood	827	189	638
All products	12,512	11,330	1,182
Logging residues	777	697	80
Other removals	40	40	0
Total removals	13,329	12,067	1,262

[1] Annual timber removals for the last decade estimated to be 13,245,000 cubic feet.

38

Table 26.--Timber removals[1] from live sawtimber on commercial forest
lands, by items, and softwoods and hardwoods, South Dakota, 1962

(Thousand board feet)[2]

Item	All species	Softwoods	Hardwoods
Roundwood products:			
Saw logs	39,742	38,568	1,174
Veneer logs and bolts	1,530	0	1,530
Pulpwood	5,508	5,508	0
Cooperage logs and bolts	0	0	0
Piling	60	60	0
Poles	2,892	2,864	28
Mine timbers	0	0	0
Posts	408	396	12
Other	2,903	2,415	488
Fuelwood	2,280	520	1,760
All products	55,323	50,331	4,992
Logging residues	3,228	2,914	314
Other removals	17	17	--
Total removals	58,568	53,262	5,306

[1] Annual timber removals for the last decade estimated to be
56,475,000 board feet.

[2] International ¼-inch rule.

Table 27.--Volume of unused residues at primary manufacturing
plants, by industry and type of residue, and softwoods and hardwoods, South Dakota, 1962

(Thousand cubic feet)

Species group and type of residues	All industries	Lumber	Veneer and plywood	Other
Softwoods:				
Coarse[1]	1,144	931	0	213
Fine[2]	1,603	1,603	0	0
Total	2,747	2,534	0	213
Hardwoods:				
Coarse[1]	89	47	42	0
Fine[2]	101	33	68	0
Total	190	80	110	0
All species:				
Coarse[1]	1,233	978	42	213
Fine[2]	1,704	1,636	68	0
Total	2,937	2,614	110	213

[1] Material such as slabs, edgings, and veneer cores.
[2] Material such as sawdust and shavings.

39

Table 28.--Projections of available cut, net annual growth, and inventory of growing stock and sawtimber on commercial forest land, South Dakota, 1962-92[1]

Species group	Growing stock (Million cubic feet)				Sawtimber (Million board feet)[2]			
	1962 (Inventory year)	1972 (Inventory year plus 10 years)	1982 (Inventory year plus 20 years)	1992 (Inventory year plus 30 years)	1962 (Inventory year)	1972 (Inventory year plus 10 years)	1982 (Inventory year plus 20 years)	1992 (Inventory year plus 30 years)
Softwoods:								
Cut	[3]13	21	31	38	[3]60	93	118	131
Growth	27	31	35	39	91	104	110	114
Inventory	1,007	1,144	1,213	1,234	3,469	3,739	3,755	3,631
Hardwoods:								
Cut	[3]1	2	2	2	[3]6	6	6	7
Growth	3	3	3	3	12	10	10	10
Inventory	78	91	105	117	247	284	319	346
Total								
Cut	14	23	33	40	[3]66	99	124	138
Growth	30	34	38	42	103	114	120	124
Inventory	1,085	1,235	1,318	1,351	3,716	4,023	4,074	3,977

[1] These projections assume that (1) There will be no major reduction in the area of commercial forest land; (2) timber will maintain its market position relative to competitive materials and demands for timber products in South Dakota will continue to increase at about the present rate; and (3) timber management will become more intensive, especially with respect to improving the number, spacing, vigor, and age class distribution of trees.
[2] International ¼-inch rule.
[3] 1962 cut estimates are trend level rather than actual.

E
)66

), 1970

ION

MP

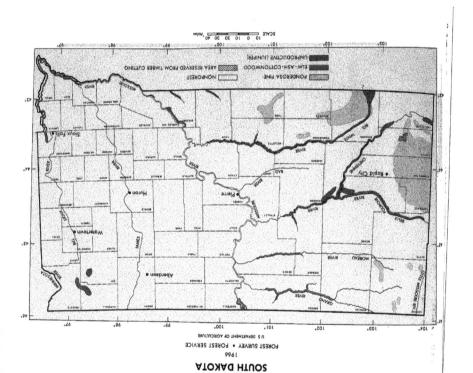

MAJOR FOREST TYPES
SOUTH DAKOTA
1966
FOREST SURVEY • FOREST SERVICE
U.S DEPARTMENT OF AGRICULTURE

2. 1962 cut estimates are trend level rather than actual.

Lightning Source UK Ltd.
Milton Keynes UK
UKHW020628060119
334855UK00006B/274/P

9 780331 394399